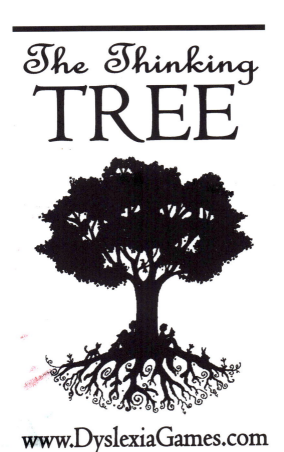

www.DyslexiaGames.com

Copyright © 2011 the Thinking Tree, LLC
All rights reserved.

**Dyslexia Games Copywork From the Bible
Friendly Copyright Notice:**

ALL DYSLEXIA GAMES, WORKSHEETS, AND MATERIALS MAY <u>NOT</u> BE SHARED, COPIED, EMAILED, OR OTHERWISE DISTRIBUTED TO ANYONE OUTSIDE YOUR HOUSEHOLD OR IMMEDIATE FAMILY (SHARING IS STEALING).

Please refer people interested in Dyslexia Games to our website to purchase their own copy of the materials.

The Thinking Tree LLC • 617 N Swope St. • Greenfield, IN 46140 • info@dyslexiagames.com • +1 317-622-8852

Copywork from the Bible

Strengthen Your Faith While Learning to Read, Write & Spell

By Sarah J. Brown
& Anna Brown

Trust in the LORD, and do good;
Dwell in the land, and feed on His faithfulness.
Delight yourself also in the LORD,
And He shall give you the desires of your heart.

Psalm 37:3-4

Name:_____ Date:_____

Name:_____ Date:_____

Have you not known?
Have you not heard?
The everlasting God, the LORD,
The Creator of the ends of the earth,
Neither faints nor is weary.
His understanding is unsearchable.
He gives power to the weak,
And to those who have no might He increases strength.
Even the youths shall faint and be weary,
And the young men shall utterly fall,
But those who wait on the LORD
Shall renew their strength;
They shall mount up with wings like eagles,
They shall run and not be weary,
They shall walk and not faint.

Isaiah 40: 28-31

Name:_____ Date:_____

Name:_____ **Date:**_____

Our Father in heaven,
Hallowed be Your name.
Your kingdom come.
Your will be done
On earth as it is in heaven.
Give us this day our daily bread.
And forgive us our debts,
As we forgive our debtors.
And do not lead us into temptation,
But deliver us from the evil one.
For Yours is the kingdom
and the power and the glory forever. Amen.

Matthew 6:9-13

Name:_____ Date:_____

Name:_____ **Date:**_____

"As the Father loved Me, I also have loved you; abide in My love. If you keep My commandments, you will abide in My love, just as I have kept My Father's commandments and abide in His love. These things I have spoken to you, that My joy may remain in you, and that your joy may be full. This is My commandment, that you love one another as I have loved you. Greater love has no one than this, than to lay down one's life for his friends." John 15:11-13

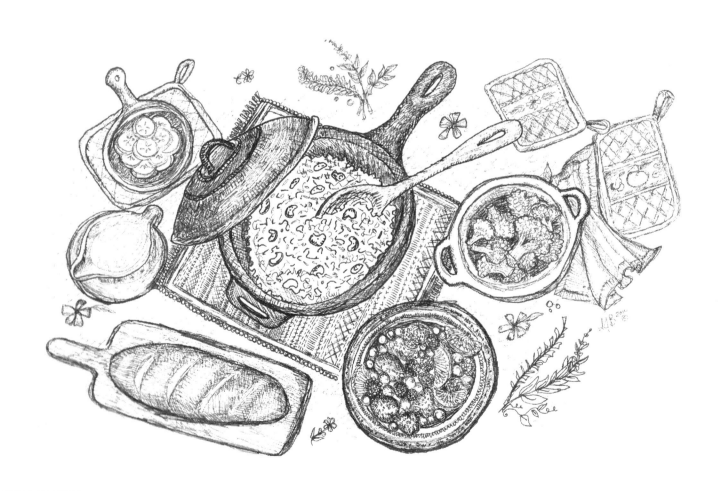

Name:_____   Date:_____

Name:_____ **Date:**_____

And we know that all things work together for good to those who love God, to those who are the called according to His purpose.

Romans 8:28

Name:_____ Date:_____

Name:_____ **Date:**_____

Trust in the LORD, and do good;
Dwell in the land, and feed on His faithfulness.
Delight yourself also in the LORD,
And He shall give you the desires of your heart.

Psalm 37:3-4

Name:_____   Date:_____

Name:_____ Date:_____

Let love be without hypocrisy. Abhor what is evil. Cling to what is good. Be kindly affectionate to one another with brotherly love, in honor giving preference to one another; not lagging in diligence, fervent in spirit, serving the Lord; rejoicing in hope, patient in tribulation, continuing steadfastly in prayer; distributing to the needs of the saints, given to hospitality.
Romans 12:9-13

Name:_____ Date:_____

Name:_____ **Date:**_____

Hear, my children, the instruction of a father,
And give attention to know understanding;
For I give you good doctrine:
Do not forsake my law.
When I was my father's son,
Tender and the only one in the sight of my mother,
He also taught me, and said to me:
" Let your heart retain my words;
Keep my commands, and live.
Get wisdom! Get understanding!
Do not forget, nor turn away from the words of my mouth.

Proverbs 4:1-5

Name:_____   Date:_____

Name:_____ Date:_____

Trust in the LORD with all your heart,
And lean not on your own understanding;
In all your ways acknowledge Him,
And He shall direct your paths.
Do not be wise in your own eyes;
Fear the LORD and depart from evil.

Proverbs 3:5-7

Name:_____   Date:_____

Name:_____ **Date:**_____

I am the good shepherd; and I know My sheep, and am known by My own. As the Father knows Me, even so I know the Father; and I lay down My life for the sheep. And other sheep I have which are not of this fold; them also I must bring, and they will hear My voice; and there will be one flock and one shepherd.

John 10 :14-16

Name:_____ Date:_____

Name:_____ Date:_____

For God so loved the world that He gave His only begotten Son, that whoever believes in Him should not perish but have everlasting life. For God did not send His Son into the world to condemn the world, but that the world through Him might be saved.

John 3: 16-17

Name:_____ Date:_____

Name:_____ Date:_____

For I know the thoughts that I think toward you, says the LORD, thoughts of peace and not of evil, to give you a future and a hope. Then you will call upon Me and go and pray to Me, and I will listen to you. And you will seek Me and find Me, when you search for Me with all your heart. I will be found by you, says the LORD.

Jeremiah 29: 11-14

Name:_____ Date:_____

Name:_____ Date:_____

Write your own favorite Bible verse on this page

Name:_____ Date:_____

Name:_____ Date:_____

In the beginning God created the heavens and the earth. The earth was without form, and void; and darkness was on the face of the deep. And the Spirit of God was hovering over the face of the waters.

Then God said, "Let there be light"; and there was light. And God saw the light, that it was good; and God divided the light from the darkness. God called the light Day, and the darkness He called Night. So the evening and the morning were the first day.

Genesis 1 : 1-5

Name:_____ Date:_____

Name:_____ **Date:**_____

How precious also are Your thoughts to me, O God! How great is the sum of them! If I should count them, they would be more in number than the sand;

Psalm 139: 17-18

Name:_____   Date:_____

Name:_____ Date:_____

Creative Copywork

Certificate of Completion

_____

Name & Age

_____

Date of Completion

The Thinking
TREE
Dyslexia Games

_____

Teacher

The Thinking TREE

www.DyslexiaGames.com

Copyright © 2011 the Thinking Tree, LLC
All rights reserved.

Created by: Sarah Janisse Brown

Made in the USA
Middletown, DE
29 May 2017